T0322365

BIRDS WITH A BROKEN WING

FICTION
Ulverton
Still
Pieces of Light
Shifts
Nineteen Twenty-One
No Telling
The Rules of Perspective
Between Each Breath

POETRY
Mornings in the Baltic
Meeting Montaigne
From the Neanderthal
Nine Lessons from the Dark

BIRDS WITH A
BROKEN WING

Adam Thorpe

CAPE POETRY

Published by Jonathan Cape 2007

2 4 6 8 10 9 7 5 3

Copyright © Adam Thorpe 2007

Adam Thorpe has asserted his right under the Copyright, Designs
and Patents Act 1988 to be identified as the author of this work

First published in Great Britain in 2007 by
Jonathan Cape
Random House, 20 Vauxhall Bridge Road,
London SW1V 2SA

www.randomhouse.co.uk

Addresses for companies within The Random House Group Limited
can be found at: www.randomhouse.co.uk

The Random House Group Limited Reg. No. 954009

A CIP catalogue record for this book is
available from the British Library

ISBN 9780224079440

The Random House Group Limited makes every effort to ensure that the papers
used in its books are made from trees that have been legally sourced from well-
managed and credibly certified forests. Our paper procurement policy can be
found at: www.randomhouse.co.uk/paper.htm

Typeset in Bembo by Palimpsest Book Production Limited, Grangemouth, Stirlingshire
Printed and bound in Great Britain by William Clowes Ltd, Beccles, Suffolk

Brighting at the five life-layers
            species, species, genera, families, order.

David Jones

CONTENTS

I

II

ACKNOWLEDGEMENTS

Acknowledgements are due to the editors of the following: *London Review of Books*, *Poetry Review*.

'The Abandoned Road' and 'Light Pollution' were commissioned for broadcast by BBC Radio 3's *The Verb* and *Between the Ears* respectively; 'The Sick Child' was commissioned by *Tate Etc.*

The Ox-Bow's Heath first appeared as a limited edition chapbook published by Ulysses (London, 1999).

The epigraph is taken from Part 1 ('Rite and Fore-time') of David Jones's *The Anathemata* (Faber, 1952), p.74. With reference to '*the five life-layers*': 'T.D. [Thomas Dilworth] points out the careful reflection of the tables printed in W.W. Watts, *Geology for Beginners* (1929), pp. 219 and 288, pages noted on the fly-leaf of D.'s copy of the book.' (René Hague, *A Commentary on The Anathemata of David Jones*, Wellingborough, 1977, p.71).

With thanks to Robin Robertson and Charles Lock.

I

BELOW ALLIHIES

Flat out, with the moor's turf in the small
of my back on the Allihies cliffs,

long before the naming of the cliffs
or of County Cork, long before the mountains

were the Slieve Mickish, to the soft interleaving
shirr of the surf against the cliff below

I drift in a half glow of sleep, then stir
awake to this westernmost view

of land edge and water and a clear sky's silica,
half not believing it, the mind's sinew

tautened by names, stiff as disagreement; then loosening
to the truth of it and losing it again.

DROMBEG STONE CIRCLE

Between the portals and the axials lay the central slab
with its slew of eurocents and hair-ties, wet-scarred words,
a Ryanair boarding pass kept from flight by a pebble.

Just when the grey rain cleared enough
to take a photograph and find the atmospherics
I'd so looked forward to, your mobile rang.

Our son in Corsica, wild-camping with a hammock
in the heatwave. You stepped to the left and the signal died.
I asked you if you'd heard his voice. 'No,' you sighed,

wondering why he'd phoned – assuming it was not
his friends who'd tried, or someone official from a ward.
You'd been standing on the line between the axials

and the portals, where the sun still casts
its westerly rays on midwinter's day above the mountain
by the sea, precise as a laser . . . so, shuttling in cross-stitch

and staring at the mobile, we searched like fallen adepts
for the place, that square foot of pulse
you'd stepped out of sync from, not quite

keeping sentinel enough. And wandering still further,
out of the stone circle and up into the heather
then worrying the track back to the gravel of car park,

it was as if we'd caught on the too-warm air
word of something dreadful that only the wise
might know how to neutralise: deciding what the offerings

should be; and who must be sacrificed, and where.

IN SYRACUSE MUSEUM

You'd have lived among them here, maybe,
left nothing more than a *BRONZE FLAME-SHAPED KNIFE*,
BRONZE HASP, *BRONZE AWL*, *BRONZE
ELBOW FINIAL* and (unevenly typed) *BONE WHORL*.

Their bronze is the verdigris brightness
of frogbit. Now what we leave
is a skein of gizmos, uncorroding;
amalgam-filled teeth; a retaliatory

stain of medicines instead of ghosts.

EARLY MORNING AT OWL'S HEAD, QUEBEC

'We are like birds with a broken wing.'
Chief Plenty-Coups, 1909

Walking the grit road
past the sign that's marked *Arrêt*

like a fish bone in an English throat
and the English names of farms

down the clear valley
where the Abenaki carried their canoes

from river to lake (and nothing
in their wake but a few

flints, the corners of glass cases
in silent rooms), with every tree

younger than the history
of our dominion here (the timber

trade), I watch the sun
clear the hill to strike

this clipped-on landscape.
Time's too savage for the long

shadows of morning to stay
longer than necessary, but the heat's

serviceable at midday after rain
when the hollows steam. I like

this loneliness, like a sharp
stone held in the palm, like the hill's

profile of Chief Owl, scarred
by ski-runs, whose shadow's

a chill I'm hurrying from
to break into sunlight, soon.

I'm sure he vowed, too, not to go down
without a fight, the day freshening

there at the edge of his woods' mind,
the red clouds scurrying from him

like all the unspoken crimes
while the neat farms still hold good down here

with their jeeps and dog-slobbered gates
and the dim, cultivated slopes beyond

like something stroked, like a still life
with its hues and shadows, the light

catching on an upright, an antenna, finally
brighting in a flash like feathers,

as if the old route's
thumped headlong

into our world-way's hurtling glass.

LIFTING THE HARP

for A

Lugging it up two flights,
three of us on the job but
my back put out as usual, I think

of what we agreed in the concert
after the course, when fifteen
of you were playing at the same

time, while Israel was pounding
Lebanon again: how if you put
a row of harpists on the front

line of any war front (each
of their hands like a lover
desperate to reach the other

through the screen of cords
over and over and never
succeeding), the guns would stop.

We reach the top and straighten up,
letting it down like a great wing, wincing
at the considerable weight it takes

to make the music of angels.

ROMAN LEAD MINES,
DERBYSHIRE

They scab the moor
where someone worked out

what they could, moved on.
Astonished ogres' mouths

bearded with nettle,
they wait for the pebble-

casting kids, their leaning
to the sound. You jumped in at the age

of five, and survived
the fall of sixty foot

unharmed, though no one
quite knows how.

If life's a field
then these are life's mistakes

stamped like hoofprints –
but one of them bore

a miracle: the boy
who sat in blackness

on a mirage of a ledge
while his father called down

not to move, descending
rung by metal rung, the plumb-line

of love acknowledged by
its own lead weight of care.

MY GRANDFATHERS' WAR

Sidney taught enfilade in Matlock –
how to fire full belt, how to receive,
how to pat the drum to swing it

from side to side: *so easily done*, he'd say.
Samuel was at Passchendaele, his younger
brother lost (killed near Arras

in the last weeks of the war), then –
shell-stunned, gassed – left by his wife.
He never saw his two small sons again

from '20 on. And yet I find in each
an equal torment: the one enthusing
lads whose bright fire life would soon

be losing (he did feel bad, he'd say);
the other mired where lines of men
would meet what Sidney meant by *easily, done*.

TWO BEIRUT POEMS

1. *Ambiguity*

1958

On a sick-making mountain drive
we were stopped by men with guns.

One waved a photo of President Chamun,
demanding our views. I was much too young

to know that if, in the hills of Lebanon
above Beirut, you got it wrong you did not live.

My father raised his hands and cried,
'Ah, mais oui . . . Chamun! Chamun!' –

not knowing they loathed Chamun, the Druze.
They only waved us to the rest of our lives

because they saw, not wild admiration,
but hands thrown up in mock despair –

and laughed and clapped as we sped from there.

2. *The Holiday Inn*

1978

Nibbled at, charred, sucked hollow by shells,
it's that shadow side of all smart hotels –

their peeling plush, the smoke in the lifts, the turd
left in the bowl by the cleaner. Life deferred.

Do the couples go on squealing through the paper walls?
Do the murmuring televisions cackle after night falls?

Snipers made secret assignations in the top suites.
Corridors filled with the dead like collected sheets.

MAIDEN FLIGHT

for J

Crouched over blueprints, slicing balsa,
the weeks it takes him erode into months
before the wing rises like a ladder

and the tissue paper stiffens. Dope
shrouds us, stings, brings thoughts.
Softly he strokes. He thinks of clouds

and the long wings against them. Sticky
as larvae they lean against the wall
of our bedroom, to dry: a draught

might blow them over. Slowly
he strokes at the crouched
chrysalis of body, then dangles into it

what, once hooked, persuades
the propellor against him. Such strength
surprises – that it doesn't

concertina into matchwood
or crumple fierily into *Hinden-*
burg. He glues the wings on

and it becomes a creature.
I trot beside him to the Dungrove field
where he turns the propellor until I want

him to stop: his finger slips
and is stropped by the blade
while the cows observe,

the wind waiting for its chance.
He lifts her high, holding her nose
as if thoughtful, hushing her, then trots

away between the crusts of pats.
His arms spread wide and she leaves
hurriedly and climbs – higher, higher

than the treetops, stops, then drops
like a stone. (I always think
of that one as the damselfly.)

FIRST KILL

A little surprised to find
the .22 was a stiffer lug
than a shelf's worth of books

after an hour of climb; more
surprised, jumping from a gate,
that the head-butt of thunder in the glen

and the glinting oyster of peat
prised open an inch from my heel
was my own doing (safety

catch left off, I was only
a boy). Surprised by the hare, literally
– there! – that popped up

from the compassless brae
and jinked its way
away through the heather, far

up-country between the peaks . . .
surprised most of all when my shot
corrected the hare's zigzag with a spin

and flung it to where I
panted up, already late, the retriever
far off on the slope below . . .

surprised, even so, to find
a hare on a tangle of meat
where the pellets had carded the rear,

its head turning in fear
but the eyes like Picasso's
countering mine with an unlidded stare:

both of us guests in bewilderment, not
really knowing quite why or how
and wondering, perhaps, if the other did?

DUBLO

1969

He handed me a tenner for my Hornby set
in answer to my notice in the corner shop:

was quiet, overweight, with spots – about
eighteen. Kneeled in my bedroom to admire,

to switch the points I'd oiled in time;
shifted the Humbrol'd personnel; adjusted

the sponge of trees. His fag fixed
smoking in the funnel, he was a bit

too old, I thought, for the large-gauge –
Double 'O' – clockwork type

that just went round, and round again
before winding down. But there was nothing

weird about him; nothing deranged.
A few days later in our local *Waitrose*,

with a shotgun hidden behind the cereal range,
he blasted the check-out girl in the face

he'd not got closer to, despite the letters.
How he just stood there, afterwards, among

the screams, I don't know. Glad, perhaps,
to be coupled to her forever now

in his own dream; our friend's friend's small twins
freckled by it in the queue.

CAPITAL

Harris, Outer Hebrides

These islands' sudden wealth was a brown wet tangle
of straps and belts, forests of it on rocks'

holdfast, slippery as the economic laws
that bound them to this the length of a war with France.

The ashes were turned into soap and glass – though this
concerned them as little as the war. Kelp

was riches, anyway, cut from its own grasp
in neap-slapped coves where seals watched them, idle,

fat with fish. The pyres' smoke sickened
the eyes with salts, though: chafed them sightless.

And it was mostly the women who slid
and struggled in the kelp's slub, wrinkled

as shamans, edged with salt; while the men surmised
on benches – backroom boys – their wives

humped it up to pyres in creels that gnawed
their shoulders, bent them old

before they were forty. Then something shifted,
like a spring tide murmuring in the lochan

from its narrow channel . . . Boney
netted. Peace with France. Resumption

of the Channel trade in cheaper (thus more profitable)
kelp. So the bullion swayed where it was, or lay

unburned in sallow mounds of stench, thick with flies.
The smoke no longer rolled over the strands.

There was a strange silence in the Sound:
no ships lay among the white flecks

the plunging gannets made, or in the gaze of the blind.
And no one brought them soap, or glass for their crofts.

No one ever brought them what the ashes made.

ON SILBURY HILL

c. 2660 B.C.

1

I'm slogging up through cow-muck once again,
flanked by tussocks and the crumbly sores of burrows.

It's artificial and there's nothing at the core –
no tomb, no gold, no secret god lying in his pots.

The slog; this moment; and memory. And love
as crisp as the air is now, if you're lucky.

2

The locals would placate it with fat fig cakes
and sugared water – though I doubt that

satisfied this mother of a belly (or suckled
breast, or gargantuan eye) with its sallow-

haunted spring at Swallowhead, quadrilled
by the OS map to something pear-shaped, dead.

3

The pivot of it all, you feel, when up
on top – though life through this early mist's

more heard than seen: chain-saws, tractors,
the cracks of a gun. No birds from the corn.

At night, of course, it's the stadium glare
of the new, executive estates; a havoc

of headlights on the A4; the marigold
smudge of Swindon foxing the stars.

4

A dag-lock of wool on a low thorn
where the peak is sinking into itself,

like a whirlpool, like a plug's been pulled
on the magic of the earth. Though perched

on this swelling, an unlikely nipple, you can think
of it all as down the shit chute. No –

as cultic, odd; a rite, a god. To which
we're proffering, not what they've found

in here (turf, antler-picks, a rusted bridle-bit)
but lands and seas and skies, and all their life.

BEFORE THE WAR

Joe Thacker, Aunt Jessie's father,
master butcher of Matlock, would sit

on his high stool at the pulpit desk
in that wallowing smell of bloodsoaked sawdust

and write out his orders with a quill
in perfect copperplate: *To*

Her Grace, the Duchess of Devonshire . . .
And then, on Saturday mornings, my not-yet father

would go in the Morris van with Len
to Chatsworth, or the Vicarage, or Haddon Hall.

Sometimes, if things got daft, he'd bicycle
off on his own, an order crammed in the pannier.

Up Haddon Hall's eternal drive
he'd pedal like the wind, to wait

in the quiet courtyard for someone
to appear (the Duke a recluse), nervous

of the rooks, the ghosts, the millstone grit
and gargoyles. Safely separate in his other hand,

bandaged in the *Matlock Times*, were the giblets,
liverlights and chitterlings, shambling already

through the match results, Chamberlain
toadying to Hitler, and all the homelier news.

BOOKMARK

More like elfin lungs
or brain biopsies than petals,

the press of ninety years
has dealt with their blush:

dull as tea stains, they spill
from my grandmother's *Poems*

of Tennyson, losing her place.
Forgotten in the attic in a box

for thirty years, the book's been mine all day,
had kept these to itself like thoughts

since 1911. And so I read, on the guarded page:
But were I loved, as I desire to be . . .

Her hair would make it to her waist
at bedtime, released from its pinned-

up bun in a silvery, fascinating stream, her door
left almost deliberately ajar –

as, by a scattering of blown red rose,
these verses might have been too, I fear.

ADDICTS

Picking at the unofficial dump, I find
a basket as spent as the fridge, the tyre,

the mangled chair. A string for a handle;
the hand that gathered chestnuts, *cêpes*,

probably bone or ash by now, judging
from the wear. Like Gogol's Plyushkin

I bring it home, place it on a sill
where it gathers the weather and frays

to a spiral nebula of reeds, half-unwoven.
Gérard spots it, four years on:

it's the type of plunder his garden's all
but buried under, the sheds so crammed

he can't get in, stuff spewing from the double doors
('I know where everything is, *mon cher . . .*')

in a slew of wares he sees himself inside,
or so he explains: today's catch could be a split

nursery spade in fluo pink, tomorrow's a car
deboned to its bonnet, motor, springs.

Not so much avarice, he says, as a cocooning urge –
the acrobatics of a '*manque maternelle*'. His wife

is threatening divorce, but he's too far gone
to change; to clear his sheds would be

to raze his mind, he suggests, gazing hungrily
at my crusts of basket, unravelling

to stems in his hand: '*Ça, c'est comme
la vie,*' he smiles, in his sardonic way…

an image I think I'll keep. A real find.

SOMEWHERE

Somewhere near Rotherham we were lost
(doubling back off the M1, cutting through)

in an area of bright, corrugated hangars
like boxes for toys; of factories wound down

to their stiff chimneys and noiseless yards
between armies of pylons, glassy business hotels,

service stations racked only to glittery
teen mags and the *Model Railway Collector*:

an anonymous, undecided England
in which the odd terraced house stood

still as its sooted brick, a stitch in a street
razed for dodgy dealerships and drive-thrus,

for roundabouts the cars attacked like wasps
while we pondered our exit, strangers here

in a land so familiar to others
it is the only view from the bridge

of their lives: limitless, boasting the future
like a suite of rooms opening one into the other forever.

PURPOSES

Fifteenth-century Bible, Montpellier

It merits more than this: two pages
open under glass, the size of a hand,

the text a wodge of black that,
like ants under a stone, reveals

itself close up as tiny curls of intent:
not a blot, not a feint. I can feel

the draughty cell, the hard wood
of the bench, but not the days themselves

he ravelled out to this – bent double
like a lover at the well of ink,

affecting his eyes. And what did he think
when he finished a double page, arrived

at the turn? A mere kink in the long
snaking way of the book, as thick

as his patience in the swelter of summer,
the frosty absence of swifts in the cold:

a sigh, perhaps, or a stir of limbs like purpose
that lies here now in its own darkness, page under page.

2

Depuis 1921

They've moved the machines: ten tons
of Heidelberg iron, hot-metal slide and punch,

towed out to leave this void in the place
I loved to linger in, watching it work,

lead and ink and the subtle, feathery press
of the sharp-set rollers, the care and expert eye

of the Barnier brothers (third generation), who read
the books. All now gone, now it's just computers.

Whose words will slide off the page in a century's time
(Michel says), just riding on the paper as they are,

not impressed, like his – which are seemingly
incised in certain lights, as if by a quill,

as if by something urgent, like a need
that merits more than this empty floor or these dusty

piles of brown-wrapped books, unclaimed for years,
that no one has either read or will ever read.

DEFEAT

in memoriam Richard France

With the backdrop of a London caff
we'd feel more real – us preened

and patted, public-school types
plotting subversion in the glory days

(a kind of green-striped red). You remember
the worker, I presume? Powdered with his wage,

weary, he'd smack the butt-end of the ketchup
or cradle the mug like a lover's face,

pouting into steam. Knew all the ropes, we reckoned –
life's block and tackle, that head for heights . . .

the struggle's hoplite, slumped on the eve
of some enormous strife. And if

our last conversation was not in a caff
but somewhere fancy with tubular chairs

and menus so thin, so tall, they couldn't
take the wind from your gestures, still

we were saving the world over breakfast
in the plunge and soar of it: your intellect

seared with passion. *Look, Ad, we've
to change our lives for once and for all.*

Something removed your retaining wall
in the few short weeks between then and when

you took to the air from a Deptford warehouse
back in '82 – high enough to matter, of course.

Since then, the silence. And no more signals (as far
as I'm concerned) but your brief, unassuming parts

in dreams – like the early roles a film star
might look shyly back on, yet grieve for.

THE OX-BOW'S HEATH

Quilhan

1

I do not say to you: illuminate me.
I lack even that confidence, that pluck.
Remind me of something that is coveted.
Your roots do not go deep. Your grass springs back.

2

A waste, a tract, a dryness, flooded sometimes.
Swallow me whole: put back the wry, the splendour.
The wry splendours of ilex, and all your shrublets.
The rough strawberries of the strawberry tree.

3

Thorniness plucks. The path shrugs thorniness off.
It snakes like this, I think, to keep its breath.
My footfalls on ling, on thyme, hush the thicket.
This is the emptiness the hunters bring.

4

Rockiness and river. Stumbling heat and plunge.
Winter, and I can watch the mountains pass.
Their snow. Their breathless rain. My hand in their
old songs burning to be sung, and to be over.

5

A grey heron's hoarse flap up, yards off.
Flood-pools of snagged trees primevally heaved from!
We should not 'lizard' the dinosaurs, I've heard.
They moved their heads like birds. They flustered lagoons.

6

Softly mudded, a boar's defiant passing.
Our clumsy pasts will always haunt us, crouched to.
By whom? By wishers-well. By men with guns.
May your bristly flanks be far. Go well.

7

We toss our sticks in, urge them. Then skip stones.
Yelping to water, you're the first one in.
Your chin slides and puts the poplars in a flap.
No throwing now! For the river bears her.

8

Aleppo pine against the deepening sky.
Triremes' prows prancing over darkened water.
Because you have no thirst, perhaps, you soar.
Aleppo pine against the sudden evening.

9

Heathland, then thickets. Poplars along water.
A field of barley like a gasp. The vines.
The ilex glitters all its classic coins.
The church, rooted out, seethes with cicada.

10

The river binds us in its sack, or *larme*.
What's wrong with ox-bow? Because it doesn't yoke us?
It does: it drives us to it through the brush.
In dreams we hear it chafe, to make all lagoon.

ON HER BLINDNESS

My mother could not bear being blind,
to be honest. One shouldn't say it.

One should hide the fact that catastrophic
handicaps are hell; one tends to hear,

publicly, from those who bear it
like a Roman, or somehow find joy

in the fight. She turned to me, once,
in a Paris restaurant, still not finding

the food on the plate with her fork,
or not so that it stayed on (try it

in a pitch-black room) and whispered,
'It's living hell, to be honest, Adam.

If I gave up hope of a cure, I'd bump
myself off.' I don't recall what I replied,

but it must have been the usual sop,
inadequate: the locked-in son.

She kept her dignity, though, even when
bumping into walls like a dodgem; her sense

of direction did not improve, when cast
inward. 'No built-in compass,' as my father

joked. Instead, she pretended to ignore
the void, or laughed it off.

Or saw things she couldn't see
and smiled, as when the kids would offer

the latest drawing, or show her their new toy –
so we'd forget, at times, that the long,

slow slide had finished in a vision
as blank as stone. For instance, she'd continued

to drive the old Lanchester
long after it was safe

down the Berkshire lanes. She'd visit exhibitions,
admire films, sink into television

while looking the wrong way.
Her last week alive (a fortnight back)

was golden weather, of course,
the autumn trees around the hospital

ablaze with colour, the ground royal
with leaf-fall. I told her this, forgetting,

as she sat too weak to move, staring
at nothing. 'Oh yes, I know,' she said,

'it's lovely out there.' Dying has made her
no more sightless, but now she can't

pretend. Her eyelids were closed
in the coffin; it was up to us to believe

she was watching, somewhere, in the end.

ANSAPHONE

She's still on the ansaphone
my father hasn't changed yet, when he says

the official bit about
'talking after the bleep'

and then turns to her to comment, letting
the tape run by mistake for a fragment

of precious sound I strain to hear
but she doesn't reply

and yet she's there.

HANDS

The young, spotty couple in *Waitrose*
held hands even while the girl

was grabbing a tin from a bottom shelf,
forcing him to bend over like a clown;

they were welded to each other.
But neither of them were blind

like my mother, for whom a hand
was a lifeline. When someone close

dies, you always wish you'd
held their hand for a little

longer than you did; it's a kind
of rule. Or you want

to have held their hand forever –
but that's impossible. I'm talking

about the realm of the real, where
regret has flesh, and interrogates:

So why didn't you take her hand
and hold it in your own for a little

longer? Or why didn't you hold it
at all? Because you don't do that

in families, after a certain age,
unless it's for a purpose – such as

helping someone over a gate
or a sudden irruption of bad news.

Especially when it's the wrong way round,
as here: not the mother comforting the child

but the child comforting the mother,
like the dying comforting the alive.

TRANSPARENT

I feel transparent.
I want to be transparent
in everything I do and say.

I want people to see
right through me, to see
fields or buildings beyond my spine,

as though I've not been
diluted so much as scanned
by some ultra-sonic ray

that has rendered everything
clotted and knotted inside me
free and floating, off and away.

This is not the same as death.
It is to do with time,
with realising one has

so little time, in the end.
It's an effect of grief, too,
to be honest. It's the solitary

floundering of someone
in the knee-deep
snow of grief, right

in the blizzard of it
and pressing on, regardless
and light-headed.

AMPURIAS

The sea's uncertain edge is all cream gloves
and sleight of hand, palming the dried-up sand

to fan this silky gleam our toes subside in.
Endless repetition's the aim, and not perfection.

Further off, a fist of foam is smacked
to flowers on the great sea-wall's surviving boulders,

Greek as Odysseus, but here in Spain;
for this was where they landed, turning the wilds

to Iberia, leaving this town with the name
my daughter asks for again, liking its sound,

like a tide's sigh hollowed by amphorae:
Ampurias.
                    Conjured one night from the dunes

by a gale, tapped by trowels, it bares its blueprint
of shops and streets like a limestone shelf

abandoned by the tide, drawn so low even
our kids can wave over it from the far side –

like Ypres after the war. There is no unpromising
quarter any more, just the grandeur of rubble,

the nice and the nasty indistinguishable
in cinerary urns and unguentaria, or heads

like marble cannonballs with neat coiffures.
The sea stayed on as people passed; the stiff

cock hewn in the ashlar wall is Roman,
we read – the white-limbed amputees

their gods with rods in. Stone, clay, rusted metal,
it might be some post-Nazi Polish *shtetl*

without the stench; or a Beaconscot-like take
on Dresden, Fallujah. Decline and fall, we think,

of course – the kids growing bored
by the fifth mosaic. I'm all but relieved

by time's thoroughness: that nothing
lasts but rock. Missed for a while

we're soon forgotten, *ultra crepidam*,
impossible to fathom. The sea-breeze brings

these honey whiffs of wild alyssum
from the bumpy, unexcavated slopes

I almost prefer: like the present moment's
phantom dunes, locking in whatever

has to come, as well as all that's past.

THE TAXI-DRIVER'S TALE

The pearly, mutton fat
of her bared thigh
was blown in sleep from its hip

through the convent glass
and came back home in a sack
swung by his dad,

lunchtime. 'His job, you see,
as a warden in the C.D.,
was to swab the decks of bits and bobs

you wouldn't want to view,
would you, going
to work the morning after a raid?

Though we
two lads were clamouring to spot
what the sack was holding that particular day,

it being all bulge.
"Curiosity killed the cat,"
was all he'd say; then,

opening up the top
to let us look: "A nun, showing
a bit of leg!"

Humour, it was, saw us through.
Nothing more to be said,
there.' I ask if anyone

close was lost – someone he knew.
'In a way,' he nods, 'in
a way.' As if

it's only now he's thought it.
The winding English lane's
frayed to the commercial estate

of car-dealerships and big-box stores
before he speaks again. Then:
'This bomb, in Finchley Road,

so all the lorries
are sent down our quiet road instead,
loads and loads all day.

And my kid brother, Ted,
on his bike,
forgets, and shoots

straight out our gate.
So, yes – in a way
it *was* the war. Our road

being ever so quiet, before.'
And nothing more
(as we arrive

at the station and I reach
for my wallet and pay)
to be said, then, just there.

INVALID

On the train out of Nuremberg
I shared a first-class carriage

with an old man who asked me to swap
seats, as he couldn't face

the direction in which the train was going
without turning faint thanks to a wound

in his head (really, a hole in which
he invited me to stick my thumb)

from a dose of shell at Stalingrad.
His fingers were burned to a claw

by frostbite; he was all raw victim –
nineteen when it happened – though German

and in the Werhmacht, then. His reward
was free travel, first class, *überall*

in Deutschland. Yes, his hole was deep
and on his skull, invisible under the hair.

A secret thing. A place where war had come
and gone, like a nightmare, like a devil's

print in stone: a tiny hoof
that left him unable to face that one direction

life rushed at him from, before plunging on.
I knew what he meant. It's easier

to sit with your back to things,
watch them glide away and dwindle

there where you've already been
into the long liquid of remembering.

IN TESCO'S

The age of reason firm against
the slight bruise of doubt,
there is something of Leibniz in these apples.

Each has been photographed seventy times
by a Greefa Intelligent Quality Sorter
for blush, for green, for blush-on-green

to the square millimetre, to the finest
per cent, then prodded, like snow, by a 'pene-
trometer' for pressure, for the hard

profit of shelf life. Like God picking
that which was (according to Leibniz)
the most perfect from an infinity

of worlds, we choose our apples
(bathed in chemicals, flown around the globe)
by uniform colour and standard size.

I remember the scrunchlings scattered
on the verge in the Corrèze, wrinkled
as bollocks, sweet as sin, with the worm

still in. *The best of all possible worlds*, we said.

EXPULSION FROM EDEN
(RESTORED)

Brancacci Chapel, Sta Maria del Carmine, Florence

His hands, bruised only
with the juice of fruits,

cover his face; hers
her nakedness, like a girl

surprised in the shower.
Later, shame of his shame

shielded them with leaves
below, like a couple

of tossed wreaths, caught mid-air.
Now a six-year sponging's

restored their all to view
and freshened the beggars

and cripples on the other wall
where a baby's bottom is bared –

the first in art! – for lack
of rags, we assume . . . Masaccio's job

was to show our wrongs
and we have merely

swabbed them to look new.

THE SICK CHILD

Edvard Munch (fourth version)

I

Perforated into a certainty
of symptoms, coughs, the only pink

her eyelids, she's gazing at the light,
hitched upright in a chair to ease

the beak-pecked bird-lungs. Her hand's all
heat, violet, relieved of the difficulty of fingers.

The mother's shucked from her spine by grief,
a doll flopped down in the execution

of prayer, under its fall of black – perhaps
comforted there, or scrabbling to recover

composure. The white is harried into life
behind, a migraine of much-too-bright

from the starched breaker of the pillow
thicker than the skull, its lantern face

turned to a window that we
will never see, out of frame as we are:

visitors with nothing to say.

2

The kept air hardly stirs, despite the curtain
drifting into shot. It is all blame

composed in blocks. It is sorrow
in splurge and clots. *My Sophie, my sister!*

we can hear it scream. Or all but, as
cut flowers do. The sternness grating on despair.

With bated breath, through the desperate
ghostings of the palette-knife

nothing can adjust, like poor reception,
I wait for her to move, unfix

from sweat and hair-loss, serene
as in Oslo in 'eighty-two, when I

fell for her in the hushed museum.
(And this is true. I was like that then.)

Now it's nearer to the juddery blur
of a home movie watched after years,

reckless with wear and tramlines:
the stuck-out tongue, that cheeky grin,

her handstands on the lawn in the sun.

TIDAL TIMES

Like invisible tennis – no racquet, no net, no ball
but each shot perfectly received and returned –

the tidal times have taken his body as she sits
at home, waiting with his final note she found

too early – early enough to save him, anyway.
As the note instructed (in this very

eventuality), she called a friend,
sat with her and some wine until

it was just too late by the tidal times
he'd carefully recorded… then gave the police a call:

she loved him too much to disobey, or to think
of racing over the sands to drag him (living) away.

A strange story, though I understand
the ebb and flow of it, the way the sea filled

his lungs like relief, like love, like a cry
to be saved and not to be dragged onto land

like a boat onto shore or a fish gasping
in impermeable air – out of his element,

say, some law transgressed as hers was not.
Though I'm uncomfortable with it, too;

such deadly love. Such disbelief
in the sweet chance of his mouth in her hair.

CUCKOO

Aunt Jessie's left me a shoebox
tight with postcards, in which

I find this view of Winster
signed (by Granny's brother, Stan),

Your loving son – West Bank
bleared to a fog through scattered girls

in pinnies; the clots of horse-muck whited out.
Can you recognise Cuckoo at the door

of Aunt Becka's shop, Stan asks
in an inky scrawl thawed out a hundred

years too late for him to presume.
My mother's hawk-eyed reading lens

she'd contrive to spy whole novels through
expands the shrub to a group

in crinoline; wipes the sign to the ACKS
of JACKSON (our family, that); unblots

a stare that moved. *Dear Father,*
Can you recognise… There's something

shaped like a wooden spoon
by the smoothed coin of face.

Did 'Cuckoo' then deserve his moniker?
Was he the village puddenhead; Winster's

prat? Stan I do recall, of course –
white-whiskered, cheery,

with a wheeze from the Somme as if
he'd run from it that afternoon.

He'd have said who Cuckoo was, but he's
long dead – as is his nephew, *Jessie's* Stan . . .

while Winster's graveyard holds these names
like yearned-for letters stuck with damp

or wonky doors jammed tight in corridors
of air: Aunt Maud lovely, died too young;

or Fred, the one the war took off
in late '19, 'his poor lungs green

from gas', my grandmother said
(who's also dead). But Cuckoo? No idea.

And who stands just before him in the door,
her pinny like a sheet pegged out to dry,

a square white sail in the sea of brown?
Is that Aunt Becka of the family shop –

her face no more than shade, and even 'Becka'
too faintly heard, like a bird

through failing light in a far-off wood?

NÎMES

I

Grand' Rue

We are eating dinner when there are three
sudden explosions . . . tighter, more concentrated

than the bangers they use in the bullfight *feria*.
Shouts, cries, a shriek of anger. We lean

out of the window to look. Someone, it seems,
has been shot. He staggers, blood-capped,

like a drunk. People watch, at a distance − a few
walk on. A thin man swerves into our narrow road

with a baseball bat, screaming, 'I'm going
to kill you, *putain*!' He runs straight past

the shot man, now gripping his knees. We don't
get who the thin one wants to kill,

but watch it all from above, bland
as cameras. When the plain-clothes

cops arrive, all yells and handcuffs,
I take a photo, but it comes out black

in the twilight. The only trace that's left, now,
is a spatter of blood like a leak of oil

and, in the window-box, the piebald pansies
our curiosity has elbowed flat.

II

Tour Magne

A broken molar on the top of the hill,
stooled by pigeons who make a dovecot of it,

dazzling in the sunlight swept by today's
mistral, it flaunts its imperial decay

in green spots of pellitory-of-the-wall,
in broken arches and a ragged crown

giddying into clouds where the look-outs once
surveyed the world as known to Rome.

It reminds me of the Pentagon. And of my son's
Czech schoolmate – a brilliant girl –

who threw herself over its rail last year,
leaving a note by her bedroom door:

You thought you knew me. I'm sorry.

LIFE CLASS

Every Friday we strive and fail
to make the comparison
between shadow and shape,

scorch of light
and charcoal scratch, hue
of flesh and the hopeless

cry of paint. We bristle
with our weaponry, kidnap,
rape. The nipple

must remain a suggestion,
eyes are never, it seems, straight.
The two-bar heater

keeps the model at the right
temperature, like
the Ice Man sunk under glass:

we thaw and freeze
onto paper, board, the drumskin
of sized canvas. The body

becomes its hollows
and awkward, meddlesome zones:
the waist does not exist, really, the legs

go on and on too long
for the feet (too big) to fit.
Four hours up and we are all

exhausted, washing our hands
like surgeons, the operation
barely even a partial success:

we blame, as ever, the cigarette
breaks – the fresh confusions
of fingers and folds, the tangled

tree-line of hair. As if a miracle
is there to be repeated again
and again, or the body's grace

to be retained for good, just anywhere.

II

THE ABANDONED ROAD

Languedoc

1

This friendlier route to the town is always clear,
chattering back in time to our steps,
loosening its stones in those places where

the rains have clawed and a slash
has grown a ravine – not quite
the end of the road but its interruption;

the buzzards spreadeagled on high,
however, their cries like peewits
or seagulls with almost nothing to say.

And even geology is never completed: the way
uppermost on granite, first, then limestone
lower down that's loosed on schist – like a rugged

list of clues, like something we ought
to have perused (while the light was good,
while we still had time) as lovers

do their bodies, revelling and astonished.

2

The last car to make it through, according to the farmer
whose car it was, was a low-slung Renault
he forced to town and back in sixty-six.

And now the road's an unpronounceable word,
the sum of its syllables – whose meaning, if not
quite lost, is known only to a few: tycho-

parthenogenesis, for instance. Or the whole
of Oc. The Homo Sapiens look, of course,
one day soon: a trace of something that tore

the ground up, was there for an aim that grew unclear
and scorned, it seems, survival – sandbagged for a while
then lost at some point no one recorded,

like a sinister bruise ignored until too late
(when you're fading away). Look, the little stream
we always drink from, where the stones give way

to rough cement the last stretch down, the echoey
barks of dogs at rusty gates, civilisation
in a washing-line and tended tomatoes,

this high old wall that seems too pompous
for its present state. Coming out now
onto the proper road by the Resistance memorial

we rest for a while – noting, of course, how
a metalled road has no real life, improved
to the point of sensing only where it has

to get to: no gingerliness. You say: *no soul*,
as if a trail of stones has soul, as if something
beyond's compressed by the bitterness of tar.

3

We turn for home, praising the rock,
the holes, the welts of mud where the water
can't quite drain. Walking back the way

you came is not like history
because you learn, not what you always knew,
but that where you've just been

is also true – refashioned already by the fresh
direction, the brilliance of the light
you're no longer facing, the different

incline, a whole new self in tow
and the one in front you can never
really know but will be, one day,

abandoned by, or in turn abandon,
though the end seems so unlikely now
on this bareness of stones, some sent askew

by our solid healthy trudge. This view.

LIGHT POLLUTION

Summer solstice, 2005

I

We're the farthest cry, today,
from the pinched waist of the year:
  nightfall in England, here, is

hardly at all, falling so late
that I remember, as a boy,
  sleeping with sunlight

still pale on the curtains,
the day not drawing its breath
  in time for dreams

so sometimes I'd wake again
before sunset, thinking it morning,
  the voice of the television's

late film, the embroidery of birdcalls
that weren't the shrill gauze of dawn's –
  and the light all wrong,

from the wrong direction, more sheet
iron than gold. Perhaps the night
  won't come (I'd think) with its

probable horrors through a summer
toss and turn, out of the longest day.
  Though it did, each time; the relay

of birdsong unceasing through
owl and nightingale to the next
  dawn that brimmed with its own

length, its scents of holiday and the end
of term and the lazy, gnat-filled evenings
   by nettlebanks or on small,

suburban lawns as large as the promise
of it all: the year half done but
   the best to come, so I did not care

if the night notched up its share
from then on in, the silent cogs
   working the pendulum's weight

the other way: to the cold of midwinter,
a dark that never quite goes away,
   to the rest and end of my life.

2

And here we are in the rest
of our lives, wanting to stay –
   which is why, perhaps, the world,

like a parched river-bed, has never
known so little darkness, they say,
   as on this summer's solstice;

for we have, like some ancient
cultic ceremony of torchlight and pyre,
   concealed our nights behind streetlamp

and floodlight, afraid of the pitch
black of the medieval room, or of woods
   strung by nothing but the moon.

Our dark side, shadowed by its sunlit half,
should be in thrall to itself, as the Earth
　　was, once – the unconscious

its own horizon, lumbering yard by yard
over forests, oceans, once a day,
　　relinquishing the light . . .

yet like a mirror ball winking and flashing
in a silent, blacked-out hall, the Earth's
　　dark side is not . . . and looks as odd

as ours must do, as if there's something
to conceal. For instance, where I recall
　　the hush of unseen fields (a dimness

of rustling trees in the darkness of air),
the retail centre's empty car park's
　　bright as a prison camp at midnight,

keeping it up all hours in a lonely glare
by the insomniac motorway. This is
　　light, not as illumination

but as caffeine, as cocaine,
cutting our nighttime streets to the bone,
　　exposing the nerve of everything that moves

or sewing open a garden's eyelids
for a barbecue laughing late among shrubs
　　as subtle, once, when they stirred after dark

as the sea under starlight, under the stars
we've drowned. We will pay in kind
　　for our blindness, one day soon –

the badgers loping over the grassed
main roads, the night sky healed
    from its bruise of sodium, and the only

clue to the lenses of the headlamps
coming from the stars, considerable again
    above the shattered carcasses of shops, offices,

or the patched lean-tos where a clutch
of you stir in your sleep, humbled survivors –
    dreaming already of appeasing

the night, as she has to be appeased:
you've found her again in yourselves.
    And she's a god outside, too, to you

who are scared, now the dogs are wolves:
a god as equal to daylight's glare
    as water to fire, as beneath to above:

sacred once more, in her own good time.

3

And the way the fragrance
of a sunwarmed track is stronger
    at night, in the blindness of it,

through the floating glimmer of parsley flowers,
it's as if we need the night to tell us
    what the day has done: in the faint

almond of bindweed, even,
or feverfew lemony underfoot
    through the wheat-like tang of cow-slop

stored with sunlight. England
in June, at night (its true
   darkness harder to fathom, now,

than when I trespassed as a boy
or lay in a field, drunk on cider,
   watching the new moon edge through a stir

of corn), wants to be left to her squeaks
of bat and owl and hedgehog,
   to what Hardy called 'some nocturnal

blackness, mothy and warm', where
ghosts can pass over the lawn –
   where your ghost, too, can.